T0009952

VITAL LIVING

walk

for a calmer you

RED WHEEL

This edition first published in 2023 by Red Wheel,
an imprint of Red Wheel/Weiser, llc
With offices at:
65 Parker Street, Suite 7, Newburyport, MA 01950
www.redwheelweiser.com

ISBN: 978-1-59003-555-9

Library of Congress Cataloging-in-Publication Data available
upon request.

Author: Becky Dickinson
Cover design: Milestone Creative
Contents design: Jo Ross, Double Fish Design Ltd
Illustrations: under licence from Shutterstock.com

Printed in China

10 9 8 7 6 5 4 3 2 1

contents

Walking is man's best
medicine.

HIPPOCRATES

introduction

There is no exercise as simple yet as effective, as gentle yet as empowering, as universal yet as personal, as walking. No other activity provides that unique, almost paradoxical combination of relaxation and exercise, firing muscles and circulation, while soothing the spirit and feeding the soul. Nothing liberates the mind quite like getting outside and simply placing one foot in front of the other. It's as if the soles of the feet take on a heartbeat of their own, settling into a familiar, reassuring rhythm that brings us into harmony not just with our surroundings, but with our inner selves.

A vigorous five-mile walk will do more good for an unhappy but otherwise healthy adult than all the medicine and psychology in the world.

PAUL DUDLEY WHITE

CHAPTER 1

let's walk

The health benefits of taking regular walks are unequivocal. Whether it's an urban march, a bucolic stroll or a mountainous hike, walking lowers the risk of all sorts of chronic conditions including heart disease, cancer, diabetes, depression and even dementia. Quite simply, the longer we walk, the longer we are likely to live. What's more, walking is invigorating without being exhausting, and it improves our fitness levels without placing our bodies under undue stress. You would be far less likely to do yourself an injury if you walked the dog every day of your life, than if you trained for just one marathon.

Yet perhaps the most profound effect of walking is the extraordinary way in which it can improve our mood and increase feelings of well-being. Walking – whether for its own sake or to reach a destination – provides a tremendous antidote to stress, releasing our minds from the cacophony of daily life and the constant demands on our attention. And when the noise stops, other things seep in: creativity, inspiration, joy, inner peace, even healing. When we allow ourselves to be led by our feet, thoughts and ideas, contemplation and conversation follow. Walking really does 'blow away the cobwebs' and it's cheaper than therapy!

What's more, there is something about moving at a human pace, without the use of machines (wearable technology aside) that reunites us with ourselves and our environment. Walking forces us to slow down and to take stock. It enables us to feel more in tune with our bodies, but it also gives us a deeper affinity for our surroundings. Whether you are tramping across fields or striding along busy sidewalks, it's amazing how much more you notice on foot than when you are stuck inside a car, or a bus. From hidden alleyways and ornate brickwork, to long shadows and sunlit leaves, it's this joint sense of familiarity and discovery that helps us to feel alive and connected to the places in which we live, work and visit.

And while walking may not be powerful in terms of speed or force, it is hugely empowering on a personal level. When we don't have to rely on anything or anyone else to get us to a destination, there is a sense of freedom and personal control. We can choose our own route, our own pace and our own view, while thinking our own thoughts.

As a form of self-powered transport, walking avoids the irritations of stoplights and rush hour; it absolves us from the misery of roadworks and public transport, and comes at no cost to the environment or our pocket. For short-haul destinations, walking is beautifully simple, convenient and accessible. But walking is so much more than a means of getting from A to B. Despite myriad advances in health and technology, science confirms what Hippocrates knew all along; that walking is man's – and woman's – best medicine. As we'll see in the following chapters, walking can enhance just about every part of our well-being, and prevent all sorts of mental and physical illnesses. From sleep aid to anti-depressant, weight loss tool to stress reliever, immune booster to heart protector, all-round mood lifter and life promoter, walking is perhaps as close to a panacea as it's possible to get.

Whether you walk to work, or walk to walk, the possibilities are limitless: increased health and happiness, adventure, inspiration and discovery. And the more you do it, the more you will discover that the journey becomes the destination. Even if it's only for 10 or 20 minutes a day, I urge you to make walking part of your life. You won't look back.

baby steps

You probably don't remember your very first steps; the tentative, faltering hope of placing one foot in front of the other, of stumbling forwards, toward a beaming parent, or a hard surface. You probably don't remember the exhilaration, the sense of freedom and surge of accomplishment of managing to stay upright while in motion. You probably don't remember hitting the ground, then getting up over and over again, until your parents lost interest. Walking then became something you just did; essential, mundane and no longer remarkable.

Most babies learn to walk sometime between their first and second birthdays. It's one of those defining childhood milestones, a moment that opens the door to endless adventures and years of costly soon-to-be-outgrown footwear. If only we could hang on to that sense of excitement; if only we could recapture the desire to keep placing one foot in front of the other, ad infinitum. Yet unfortunately, as we grow up, walking is easily neglected in favor of things that are quicker, easier or ostensibly more exciting. And when walking becomes a chore – something you need to do, rather than something you choose to do – it loses the fascination and allure it held in infancy.

Humans have been walking for millennia. Our ability to move on two legs while standing up straight is one of the things that sets us apart from other animals. Yet walking is so much more than a by-product of evolution, or a mere means of getting around. On a purely physical level, walking plays a vital role in maintaining and restoring health. Before gyms and Lycra, tramping across fields and fens would have been a primary means of exercise, helping to stave off excess weight, while keeping the blood and oxygen flowing. During the Victorian era, the 'constitutional walk' was a daily ritual (like going to the restroom) that was widely accepted as being beneficial for one's physical makeup and general health. Today, we would probably call it wellness.

However, despite the 21st-century obsession with well-being, walking seems to have fallen out of fashion. We have become time-poor and technology-dependent. Why leave the house when you can find almost anything you need on the internet, and then have it delivered? Why use your feet to get anywhere when there are buses, trains and cars?

However, with soaring levels of stress, obesity, diabetes and other chronic conditions, coupled with rising amounts of time spent in front of screens, there are more reasons than ever to get back to basics, and to move in the way in which we were designed to move. Walking doesn't just help us to stay alive; it helps us to feel alive, too. And while it can be a relatively slow way of getting from one place to another, that is what makes walking such a pleasurable and powerful experience. Walking at a human pace makes us feel, well, human. It makes it feel good to be alive, grateful for the ability to move. Instead of hurtling through life at supersonic speeds, there is a sense in which walking brings us back into step with ourselves, providing a much needed space in which we can think, heal, plan, dream, and reflect. As a means of locomotion, walking gives us a chance to compose ourselves before arriving at our destination. If you haven't yet rekindled the thrill of those first defining steps, pull on some sensible shoes, open the door and find out for yourself.

how to walk

Beyond the realms of toddlerhood, walking is something most of us who are lucky enough to be able to walk unaided, or walk at all, take for granted. The beauty of walking lies in its simple efficiency, yet the mechanisms behind this everyday activity are surprisingly complex, so why not spend a moment now checking your technique?

check your posture

We are often reminded about the importance of good posture when sat at a desk, but it's a key feature of walking, too. Start by relaxing your shoulders, keeping them back and down. At the same time, keep your back straight with your chest slightly lifted. This prevents you from slumping or slouching forward, minimizing the strain on your back. Meanwhile, your hips should be level, knees pointing forwards and your pelvis tucked under your torso.

mind your head

Your head should be centered over your torso with your chin slightly elevated. Pull your chin in slightly so that your neck is in a neutral position and your eyes are looking ahead, rather than down at the ground. This supports the head, and avoids placing undue pressure on the intervertebral discs, which helps to prevent postural pain.

strike the ground

When striking the ground, your heel should be the first part of your foot to make contact. This allows it to act like a mini shock absorber, minimizing the impact through the other joints, especially the knees. As you step, roll your foot forward, heel-to-toe, as if you are peeling it off the ground. Then push off your toes, propelling yourself forward onto the heel of your other foot. As you walk, keep your stride natural and rhythmic, and avoid steps that are too long, as this can lead to injury.

get into the swing

As you walk, your arms should begin to swing in small arcs in time with the opposite leg, to help balance your body. The quicker you walk, the larger the arcs. This increases the efficiency of your stride, helping you to walk faster and further. So, hands out of pockets and swing away. Don't worry, you won't look stupid! And remember to keep your arms by your sides with your elbows bent.

did you know?

In 2011, Canadian Jean Beliveau completed a 46,600-mile walk around the world covering 64 countries. It took him 11 years and two months.

Walking at a constant speed of 5kmph, it would take just over nine years to reach the moon.

You would need to walk for 1 hour and 43 minutes to burn off a 540-calorie Big Mac. (Or you could not eat the Big Mac and still go for a walk!)

The average person walks three times around the equator during their lifetime. Although obviously most of us don't actually walk around the equator.

Race walking is an official Olympic sport. It was introduced in 1904 as part of the decathlon, and became an event in its own right in 1932. There are 20km races for both men and women, and 50km races for men only. It's harder than it looks, but that doesn't stop people making jokes about it.

Walking on a rough but level track requires 50 per cent more energy than walking on a paved road.

Walking is the best possible exercise. Habituate yourself to walk very far.

THOMAS JEFFERSON

CHAPTER 2

walking for health

Around the world, experts agree: walking is good for you. Yet despite all the evidence pointing to the benefits, millions of people don't walk enough. Regular walking soothes stress, improves your mood and reduces the risk of numerous conditions including heart disease, dementia and cancer. These may seem like lofty claims for something as unscientific as going for a walk. Yet according to the World Health Organization, a lack of physical activity is now the fourth leading cause of death worldwide. The blunt truth is that we need to move more, and the easiest and most effective way to do this is to walk.

It's no surprise that an increasing reliance on vehicles, machines and technology to do the things that once required physical effort means that exercise levels in high-income countries have dropped dramatically over the past few decades. A lack of physical activity has become a pandemic situation. Insufficient exercise is now one of the leading causes of mortality around the world – after high blood pressure, tobacco use and high blood glucose – increasing the risk of death by between 20 and 30 per cent.

The World Health Organization states that one in four adults around the world fail to achieve the minimum amount of activity recommended for good health. Even more worryingly, more than 80 per cent of adolescents aren't active enough, putting themselves at risk of chronic diseases in the future. In the UK for example, the current generation of children is said to be the "least active generation in history," with fewer than 50 per cent of students walking to school, compared to 70 per cent a generation ago. But the good news is the declining level of physical activity around the world is something that can be reversed.

So how much exercise do we need to in order to stay healthy? The World Health Organization and other health bodies recommend that all adults between the ages of 18 and 64 should do at least 150 minutes of moderate aerobic activity per week. (For children, it's at least 60 minutes of moderate to vigorous physical activity per day.) And while 150 minutes might sound like a lot to squeeze in to a busy schedule, this works out at just five brisk 30-minute walks a week – although of course anything more would be even better.

Numerous scientific studies have shown that walking is one of the best ways to boost health and improve life expectancy. An overwhelming amount of research proves that this most humble method of locomotion can lower high blood pressure, high blood sugar and high cholesterol, and keep blood vessels healthy, reducing the likelihood of numerous diseases. Walking strengthens the heart and lungs, improves circulation and increases our general fitness.

But the benefits don't stop there; walking and other forms of physical activity also provide protection against various forms of cancer, including breast and colon cancer. Walking can also aid healthy digestion, as movement on the outside helps keep things moving on the inside, which in turn helps to prevent potentially harmful waste from building up in the colon.

In addition, walking is critical for muscles, bones and joints, as well as coordination and balance. As a weight-bearing exercise, walking promotes bone density which is especially important as we get older, as bone mass starts to diminish after the age of around 50. Walking regularly is an effective way of reducing the risk of fractures and osteoporosis.

When it comes to looking after your joints, walking can also ease symptoms of arthritis, stiffness and inflammation. Although it might sound counterproductive to go for a walk if you are suffering from knee pain, walking can actually make things better. This is because the cartilage that is found in the knee and other joints doesn't have a direct blood supply, so relies on joint fluid for nutrition. Walking gets that fluid circulating, and the compression and decompression of your body weight sends oxygen and nutrients into the area. This explains why joints may be stiff in the morning, but can loosen up once you start moving. At the same time, walking builds muscles – this takes the pressure off your knees and other joints and helps to keep them mobile.

Research also shows that regular daily walking triggers an anti-aging process and helps to repair old DNA, potentially adding up to seven years to your life. So forget plastic surgery, walking could also provide the key to staying youthful. And of course, one of the best things about walking is that it involves no training, no special skills or talent; just left, right, left, right and swing your arms.

the evidence

Study after study has demonstrated that walking is one of the best ways to look after your physical and mental health. For example, research carried out by Public Health England found that just ten minutes of brisk walking a day reduced the chances of an early death by up to 15 per cent, with further benefits for those who walked even more. In case you are wondering, a brisk walk is defined as anything above 3 miles an hour. Another German study found that walking for 25 minutes a day adds an extra three to seven years to a person's life span – even when taking into account other factors like smoking and obesity.

Many of the health benefits stem from the way that walking gets the blood pumping without putting undue strain on the cardiovascular system. Numerous studies have confirmed that taking regular walks protects against heart disease and strokes. In fact, some studies suggest that brisk walking may even be better for you than running. Scientists from the Lawrence Berkeley National Laboratory in California compared data from two studies of more than 33,000 runners and more than 15,000 walkers over a period of six years. They discovered that for the same amount of energy used, the walkers reaped greater heart benefits than the runners, and in some cases the risk of heart disease, high blood pressure and high cholesterol was reduced by nearly twice as much.

The resounding conclusion from an abundance of research is that walking won't just enhance your life, it will also prolong it and may even save it. All we need to do is put the theory into practice.

nine small ways to walk more every day

The advice has become so familiar that we have become almost deafened to it. You know the kind of thing: get off the bus one stop earlier, walk to work, buy a treadmill-powered TV. Ok, maybe not that one, but you get the gist. And while the suggestions can sometimes feel trite, there is no denying that in an increasingly sedentary and disease-burdened society, most of us need to sit less and move more. You might not be able to fit in a brisk 5km before work (although even that might be more doable than you think) but there are all sorts of other ways we can notch up a few more steps. And as that other well-worn phrase goes, it's the little things that count. So here are a few ways to walk a little more.

1. Step away from your inbox

We have become so reliant on email and instant messaging as a primary means of communication, that it has become almost second nature. However, instead of automatically pinging off an email to a colleague or anyone else within a few hundred meters, walk over to talk to them instead. The steps involved will soon add up.

2. Always. Take. The. Stairs.

Yes, it's been said before, but unless you have a pushchair or an exceptionally heavy shopping bag, there is really no reason to take the elevator. And by the time you've waited for one to arrive, the stairs will get you there in almost the same amount of time. So use your legs, and save the elevators and escalators for people who really need them. What's more, you won't be forced to inhale other people's flatulence and garlic breath, and you won't be trapped inside a small metal container in the event of a power cut. Just in case you needed any added incentive.

3. Park somewhere inconvenient

It doesn't matter if it's a grocery store, school, place of work, hospital or even a gym, trying to park as close as is physically possible to any given entrance has become something of a competitive sport. However, there are no prizes for getting the prime spot, other than perhaps a few disgruntled glares – and if you are really unlucky, a scratch on your car door. So why not avoid the scrum and park somewhere else instead? Opt for the back of the car park where you'll have much less trouble finding a space, or even a local street. As long as there are no restrictions in place, you could save money on parking fees at the same time as clocking up some extra steps.

4. Drink more

Apart from the more widely proclaimed benefits to your kidneys, complexion and general health, drinking more fluids can get more than just your bladder moving, thanks to all those extra loo trips. Just make sure those fluids are water, rather than anything fizzy or alcoholic. The standard advice is about six to eight glasses a day.

5. Take regular breaks

Unless you are a mailman, mailwoman, or door-to-door salesperson, these days there aren't many jobs that involve a great deal of walking. So if you spend hours sitting behind a desk, it's vital to take regular breaks. Unfortunately, office culture often dictates that we must be seen to be working every minute of the day and beyond. However, try to get up every 20 minutes for a quick stretch or a drink of water. Not only does this make you more productive, but it also helps to prevent back problems caused by sitting in the same position for too long. Better still, use your lunch break to go for a walk. As well as upping your daily step count, research shows that this habit also helps to reduce work-related stress.

6. Walk to school

It's not just adults who are becoming increasingly inactive, but children too. Given that many children – especially those of elementary school age – attend schools within a mile or two of their home, it's a sad reflection of modern life that fewer than ever make the journey on foot. Of course, it's not always possible to walk to school; children are tired, the weather is irritable, you need to get to work – but even walking half way or walking once or twice a week is better than not walking at all, and better for the planet. It's worth making the effort, not just for your own health, but as a way of instilling good habits in children, too.

7. Drive one way, walk the other

If you make the same journey twice in one day, such as to school, and don't need the car in between, then why not drive in the morning, leave the car there so you can walk home, then walk back again in the afternoon when you can collect the car and drive back? Similarly, if you usually drive to work – and don't have miles to go – you could leave the car overnight at your workplace and walk home on certain days. The following morning you would walk to work again, then drive home at the end of that day. With a bit of forward planning, there may be more opportunities to walk than it first appears.

8. Walk and talk

Have you ever worked out how many hours you spend on the phone, both at home and at work? Or how much time you spend in meetings, sitting on a chair? But there is no reason to sit down just because you are on the phone, or even in a business meeting. Try holding your next conference or conversation outdoors, so you can talk and walk at the same time. Just make sure you pick somewhere safe and quiet, like a park. The combination of fresh air, change of scenery and increased blood flow to the brain is likely to lead to a far more productive meeting than a soporific board room. What's more, walking is also known to spark creativity.

9. Don't just stand there

You know the saying: 'you wait ages for a bus, then three turn up at once.' Well, don't just wait, walk! Start by walking to the next bus stop, and if there is still no sign of a bus, walk to the next one. Before you know it, you may have actually reached your destination – and will have avoided the particular fury that is waiting for a bus that never shows up.

did you know?

You burn calories two to three times faster climbing stairs than you would walking briskly on level ground.

In Italy, the art of taking an early evening walk is a long-held social ritual, known as 'la passeggiata', from the verb, passeggiare, meaning to walk. The tradition still takes place in almost every town, city and village, and resembles a kind of social parade as Italians take to the streets to walk, chat and be seen.

Basiphobia is the fear of not being able to stand and walk.

A somnambulist is someone who walks in their sleep.

A perambulator is an old-fashioned word for a pram/stroller, and also means a person who walks, especially for pleasure and in a leisurely way.

You use around 200 muscles every time you take a step.

In the US, a survey found that 26% of adults sit for more than eight hours a day.

If I could not walk far and fast, I think I should just explode and perish.

CHARLES DICKENS

CHAPTER 3

walking for fitness

Forget Zumba and spin, personal trainers and hot yoga. As well as being great for heart health and disease prevention, walking is also a fantastic way to burn calories and stay in shape, without the need for fancy clothing, expensive equipment or shouty gym instructors. If you think this sounds too good to be true, then luckily, science suggests otherwise. Research shows that regular walking is a better defence against obesity than any other kind of activity. So what are you waiting for? Get your shoes on and get moving.

Physical activity is defined as any bodily movement that is produced by skeletal muscles and uses energy. This could be anything from vacuum cleaning the stairs to mowing the grass, riding a unicycle or playing soccer in the park. In other words, pretty much anything that doesn't involve slouching over a desk or sitting on a couch eating popcorn.

Yet when it comes to fitness, walking is often glaringly overlooked in favor of other more overtly 'sporty' or glamorous activities. Perhaps this is partly because walking is often viewed as a mere means to an end, an act of drudgery, rather than a path to fitness.

Furthermore, there is a commonly held perception that in order to be effective, an activity must be difficult, strenuous or beyond the capabilities of the masses. Why bother with something as simple and unremarkable as walking when everyone else is training for triathlons or twisting their limbs into slip knots?

Walking lacks the bravado of marathons and triathlons, and doesn't have the Instagram factor of yoga and pilates. You would be hard-pressed to find a sunset shot of a walker, posing in front of a temple wearing spray-on leggings with the caption 'namaste,' racking up 'likes' on social media. When it comes to walking, there is no hype or vanity, just perhaps a quiet evangelism among those who have already discovered its power.

While levels of obesity and inactivity continue to soar, at the other extreme – or perhaps as a reaction to it – are the ultra-exercisers, the fitness fanatics for whom exercise is all about adrenalin, sweat and protein shakes. And while the saying 'no pain, no gain' may inspire those seeking medals or recognition, it's more likely to leave the rest of us feeling lazy and incapable, deterring us from doing anything more strenuous than tying our own shoelaces. Because what is the point of embarking on something that seems completely unachievable from the outset?

The sight of sinewy runners in their high vis vests and expensive footwear training for their twenty-third marathon, can make something as painless and unassuming, as timeless and uncomplicated as walking, appear a bit lame in comparison. It would be easy to assume that anything that doesn't result in blisters and bleeding nipples is a waste of time.

Yet the reality is quite the opposite, and it can come as a joyous relief to discover that you don't need to run marathons – or even half marathons – or sign up to boot camp, kick boxing or circuit training – or anything else that involves obscene levels of grunting and panting, to get enough exercise. You don't even need to join a gym (unless you actually want to) – all you need to do is walk!

Walking may not be having a moment on Instagram,

but the rewards are likely to last much longer than the latest YouTube sensation. Better still, walking is an activity that anyone blessed with a functioning pair of limbs can take up, regardless of training or even time.

But can something as easy and as pain-free as walking really help us stay in shape? Surely only high-octane workouts can do that? Well the good news is that despite outward appearances, walking is an excellent way to stay lean and svelte. Not only does it help stave off disease on the inside, but it helps us to look good on the outside too. This in turn is a recipe for confidence and self-esteem.

In one study, scientists from the London School of Economics examined the activity levels of 50,000 adults for 13 years, and found that brisk walking was a more effective deterrent against obesity than any other type of exercise. The participants were divided into different groups, including those who walked regularly and those who took part in more vigorous sports including cycling, gym workouts, dancing, running, soccer, rugby, badminton, tennis and squash. And guess what? The people who walked briskly for more than 30 minutes were found, on average, to have lower BMIs and smaller waists than everyone else who took part in the study. Great news for anyone who is loathe to step on a treadmill. What's more, unlike almost every other sport, walking is something that can be fitted into daily life, meaning it's something you are likely to continue with for as long as you are physically able.

the premier league of walking

If there is one global truth about walking, it's that we do far less of it than our ancestors. However, the amount we walk varies considerably from country to country.

In the largest ever study into human movement, researchers from Stanford University tracked smartphone data from more than 700,000 people. They found that people in Hong Kong are the most active in the world – with an average of 6,880 steps a day. Mainland China came second with 6,189 steps, followed by Ukraine, then Japan, Russia, Spain and Sweden. Indonesians were reported to be the least active, managing an average of just 3,513 steps a day.

Around the world, the average number of daily steps taken was 4,961 – equivalent to two and a half miles or four kilometers. By comparison, the average British person clocks up 5,444 steps per day, while the average America manages 4,774 daily steps. The research was published in the journal Nature in 2017.

walking versus running

up a few miles. All you need is a pair of comfortable shoes and possibly some decent waterproofs.

Weather aside, there is little not to love about putting one foot in front of the other as a means of getting the blood and the body moving, getting from A to B or just grabbing some time out. Many would argue the same can't really be said about running. Just compare the commonly observed runner's grimace to the walker's expression of rosy-cheeked contentment. There is of course the satisfaction of being able to run the kind of distances usually reserved for horses, but the same can be said of walking long distances, too – minus the splintering pain and breathless sweat-drenched exhaustion.

Despite the more leisurely pace and reduced torture levels, walking isn't simply a slower or lazier form of running. Regardless of how quickly you walk (or how sluggishly you run) there is a key difference: when you walk, at least one foot is always on the ground, whereas running requires both feet to be in the air at some point during your stride. Running is in effect a series of little jumps from foot to foot, and the faster you go, the more time you spend airborne between strides.

Running is also much more high impact than walking, with each step creating a force of up to three times the runner's body weight, compared to a force of only 1.2 times body weight for walking, making it much more gentle. Consequently, running has a far higher turnover of injuries, especially to the lower body joints, including the hips, knees and ankles.

Research suggests that 20 to 70 per cent of runners will experience some sort of exercise-related injury – to say nothing of blisters and bleeding nipples, and the marathon runner's worst nightmare – jogger's diarrhea. Walking, on the other hand, carries an injury risk of around one per cent.

There is one capacity in which running beats walking hands (or feet) down though, and that's calorie expenditure. Quite simply, the harder and faster you exercise, the more calories you burn. And as running requires more effort than walking, you burn more calories. So for example, a 73kg (11 and a half stone) person would burn approximately 374 calories when walking for an hour at a speed of four miles per hour. The same person running for an hour, at a speed of seven miles per hour, would burn around 835 calories, which also means they are more likely to lose weight.

'Ah, but what about fat?' you might ask. There is the argument that walking burns fat, while running uses carbohydrates. It's true that high intensity or cardio-type exercises require quick energy, so the body grabs hold of any available carbs, which are easier to convert than fat, which needs breaking down into different components. Walking on the other hand isn't so demanding, so the body uses a greater proportion of fat as its main fuel source.

However, the bottom line is it doesn't really matter whether calories come from fat or carbohydrate. When it comes to weight loss, what matters most is the total number of calories you burn. And as running burns more calories than walking, you are more likely to lose weight. What's more, obsessing over calories represents a distinctly unhealthy and joyless approach to health and fitness. There are of course many more reasons to exercise than to drop a dress size – although losing weight may actually occur as a welcome side-effect anyway.

Furthermore, it's not all about short-term gains, or losses. As the London School of Economics study into obesity shows, it's the people who walk day in, day out who are the most likely to avoid obesity. This may well reflect the fact that walking is so blissfully simple and genuinely enjoyable, that it ends up becoming something you do for life. On the other hand, an exercise that carries a high risk of injury or pain, or requires a large amount of willpower, is much more likely to be met with an early retirement.

Ultimately, both running and walking can significantly improve your health, and there is no wrong or right way to exercise. The most important thing is to do something that you love and to do it on a regular basis. So while running does burn more calories, walking is also an excellent way to stay fit and healthy – and is for many people, far more pleasurable. So if you prefer to keep one foot in contact with the ground at all times, then just walk. And if you need to lose weight, then just walk a little further and a little faster. What's more, if you want to increase the burn without actually breaking into a jog, then there are plenty of ways to up the tempo, as we are about to find out.

seven ways to raise the intensity of your walk

While a quick daily walk is a great foundation for health and happiness, once you are doing this on a regular basis, you might want to step things up a bit for even greater benefits. The good news is this doesn't have to involve swapping your walking shoes for a pair of running trainers.

While jogging may seem like the natural progression from walking, there are plenty of other ways to raise your heartbeat, while still keeping one foot firmly on the ground. Of course, you don't need to treat every walk as a workout – there is much to be said for a leisurely, contemplative plod, too. But for those occasions when you want something a little more vigorous without actually stepping inside a gym, here are some great ways to pimp your stride.

1. Pick up the pace

As obvious as it sounds, the easiest way to take your walk to the next level is simply to go further in the same amount of time. So if you usually walk one mile in half an hour, try walking one and a half miles. Better still, try walking for an hour at that pace.

2. Take the rocky road

Walking on a smooth, flat surface uses less energy than tramping across rough, uneven terrain. So look for more challenging tracks and trails as well as hills, gradients, steps and stairs. Small variations can increase your heart rate and make your muscles work harder.

3. Throw in a few moves

Ok, you might not want to do this while walking to work amidst a sea of commuters, but for green space walks, try spicing things up with a few squats or lunges, or borrow a park bench for a few press-ups. Bodyweight exercises are a good way of building lean muscle and burning calories. Feel free to ignore any onlookers.

4. Add weight

Heavier people burn more calories. That's not an excuse to eat as you walk, but rather an incentive to carry a little extra load on your journey. This could include ankle or hand-held weights, a couple of water bottles, a weighted vest or just a rucksack, which of course has the added benefit of providing somewhere to deposit extra clothing or snacks. If you have small children and your back is up to it, then try swapping the pushchair or stroller for a baby carrier instead. Adding any kind of additional weight to your walk increases the resistance, so your muscles need to work harder, which helps to build strength.

5. Turn up the power

Not to be confused with race walking (the wiggly one), power walking resembles an exaggerated form of walking. The technique involves walking at an energetic, rapid pace, while pumping the arms back and forth. Although some power walkers can achieve speeds that are equal to or faster than jogging, one foot needs to be in contact with the ground at all times, to avoid breaking into a run.

Getting the correct arm technique is key. Keep your shoulders relaxed and swing your arms at your sides with your elbows bent at around 90 degrees. Avoid bringing the arms across the body, but move them backwards and forwards past your hips, and swing your elbows no higher than your breastbone.

As well as increasing fitness, regular power walking tones the buttocks, thighs, hips, shoulders, upper back and abs, and also speeds up your overall metabolic rate, helping to prevent long-term weight gain.

6. Pick up some poles

For the ultimate way to transform an ordinary walk into a full-body workout, look no further than Nordic walking. Originating in Finland where it was first used by cross-country skiers to maintain fitness and endurance during the summer season, Nordic walking uses 90 per cent of the body's skeletal muscles and burns almost twice as many calories as ordinary walking. It's now one of the fastest growing activities in the world, and is also surprisingly low-impact. The technique involves propelling yourself along using a pair of poles as additional legs. When used correctly, the poles increase the use of the upper body muscles, ensuring they work as hard as the legs, while also activating the core. Although the poles increase the level of exercise, they reduce the weight on the knees and lower body joints, so there is minimal stress on the body. Nordic walking isn't difficult to learn; however, to make sure you adopt the correct technique, it's best to start with a qualified instructor, or join one of the ever-growing numbers of classes.

7. Mix it up

While walking is one of the easiest and most convenient forms of exercise, for maximum physical rewards, you need to push yourself. One of the most effective ways to achieve this is by doing something called Interval Walking Training. This involves walking as fast as you can for a few minutes, then slowing down for a few minutes, then walking fast again, and so on.

This style of intense exercise broken up by periods of recovery is usually associated with the more intimidating kind of HIIT classes and gruelling fitness videos – the ones that claim you can transform your body in a matter of weeks. Such claims are not wholly unfounded – research shows that alternately raising and lowering the heart rate burns more calories than keeping it at a steady pace. The good news is you can do this without busting a gut (or a ligament) simply by swapping your steady walking pace for a combination of gentle strolling and speed walking. This boosts your calorie and fat burning potential without putting your body under too much extra stress and strain. Research has also shown that it can significantly improve your fitness levels.

In one large Japanese study, one group of walkers between the ages of 44 and 78 were put on an interval training program, where they had to perform repeated sets of three minutes of fast walking, followed by three minutes of slow strolling. The effort level for the fast walking had to be at least seven on a scale of one to ten. The total workout lasted about 30 minutes and was done at least four times a week. Meanwhile, a second group of participants were required to walk at a continuous, moderate pace – an effort level of five out of ten – for 60 minutes, four days per week.

After five months, the interval walking group showed significant improvements in aerobic fitness, leg strength and blood pressure, but those in the second group showed almost no change – pretty convincing results. These findings have been repeated by other studies, with some seeing increases in aerobic power (an indicator of fitness) by as much as 27 per cent, as well as improved blood pressure and blood glucose levels.

So for the gain of HIIT without the pain, slotting some interval training into your regular walks could be a great option. Depending on your current fitness level, try to push the intensity of the fast walking phase to the point of discomfort for the full three minutes, so that it would be hard to hold a conversation.

Remember, each intense bout is followed by an easy one, so you can catch your breath and recover during the following three minutes. Alternatively, there are lots of interval training apps that can monitor your pace, distance and exertion levels. The other great thing about interval walking is that for busy people, just 30 minutes a few times a week can bring measurable results. This also throws into dispute the whole question of whether we really need to walk 10,000 steps a day. Talking of which:

is there really a magic number?

10,000 steps has become the holy grail of walking; a daily milestone of wellness and vitality, rewarded by a rather satisfying little buzz. The pursuit of this pre-ordained number has also become something of a cultural obsession, appealing to both tech nerds and the health conscious alike, huge legions of whom have become fixated on the telling little bands around their wrists, which are now as common as tattoos, and often more expensive. It was predicted that by 2020, there would be 500 million wearable fitness trackers in use around the world.

But there is one problem: unlike other health markers – blood pressure, BMI and pulse rate for example – the 10,000 steps barometer is an entirely arbitrary number.

It was conjured up as part of a successful Japanese marketing campaign in the wake of the 1964 Tokyo Olympics. Cashing in on the ripple effects of the games, the company, Yamasa, devised an early pedometer called a Manpo-Kei, which literally translates as "10,000-step meter" from the Japanese "man" for 10,000, "po" for steps and "kei" for meter.

Since then, the now ubiquitous figure has been adopted as a popular target for physical activity around the world, and has even been endorsed by various public health bodies. We have diligently accepted that we must take 10,000 purposeful steps – the equivalent of around five miles a day – just as we must get eight hours of sleep a night and at least five portions of fruit and veg a day.

However, while walking offers huge, unquestionable benefits, especially in a sedentary, technology-driven world, there is less evidence to say that we must walk 10,000 steps a day – or even bother counting at all. In fact, the main beneficiaries may be the companies that continue to churn out these must-have devices, in assorted styles and colors.

For a start, not all steps are equal. You could walk 10,000 steps at a snail's pace or 5,000 steps at a powerful stride. It's not just how far you go, but how long it takes, and whether you raise your heart beat and get a little out of breath that counts. As studies into interval training demonstrate, it's often a question of quality over quantity.

Ultimately though, the best measure of a walk is how it makes you feel. There is a danger that by turning walking into just another set of statistics, we detract from its intrinsic value and uncomplicated appeal. Walking embodies a beautiful sense of freedom, and this is something that feels increasingly under threat in the current obsession with targets. Fitness trackers can perhaps provide a source of motivation; they can remind us of the need to keep moving and reveal our progress or shortcomings. But do we really need a machine to tell us we spend more time on our backsides than our feet?

Walking is one of those rare and blissfully non-competitive activities where there is no pressure to perform or to succeed. Do we really need to be held accountable for every step we take and made to compete, even with ourselves, for hollow validation and a pat on the wrist vibration?

Walking: the most ancient exercise and still the best modern exercise.

CARRIE LATET

Everywhere is walking distance if you have the time.

STEVEN WRIGHT

did you know?

American trekker, Steve Newman, holds the record for being the first person to walk around the world solo. Starting in 1983, it took him four years, during which time he crossed 20 countries and walked 15,000 miles.

The record for the longest unbroken walk is held by the British adventurer, George Meegan. He walked from the southern tip of South America to the northernmost part of Alaska, covering 19,019 miles in 2,425 days, starting in 1977 and finishing in 1983.

The men's world record for the 20km race walk is held by Yusuke Suzuki. It took him 1 hour, 16 minutes and 36 seconds at the Asian Race Walking Championships in his home town of Nomi, Japan.

Starting in 2003, a British man named Stephen Gough, known as the 'Naked Rambler', walked the length of Great Britain from Lands' End to John o' Groats completely naked.

The average US teen is said to be no more active than the average 60-year-old.

It is the one way of freedom. If you go to a place on anything but your own feet, you are taken there too fast, and miss a thousand delicate joys that were waiting for you by the wayside.

ELIZABETH VON ARNIM

CHAPTER 4

walking for happiness

Besides getting the heart pumping, blood flowing and muscles moving, walking soothes and restores the mind in a way that goes far beyond the physical benefits, and much further than the distance covered. As an act of self-care, getting outside for a walk is one of the easiest ways of shaking off negative thoughts and creating a positive change in your mood. In addition, there is evidence to suggest that walking may help boost cognitive brain function and reduce the deterioration of brain tissue as we age. Quite simply, walking will make you not just healthier, but happier, too.

There are two aspects of human activity that are central to happiness, health and well-being. As well as helping to improve physical health and prevent disease, numerous studies have recorded a clear correlation between walking and positive mental health. Like other forms of exercise, walking provides a proven mood-lifting effect, including the ability to alleviate depression and reduce stress and anxiety.

Of course, anything that distracts us from our day-to-day worries or provides a change of scene can have a positive effect. When faced with the relentless pressures of work, deadlines, family commitments and difficult life events, it's important that we take time out for ourselves. Going for a walk provides the perfect opportunity for a bit of 'me' time, without the pressure of going to the gym or engaging in any kind of competitive sport, or the need to spend money.

But walking is about more than just switching off from the world for a short period of time. Unlike, say, meeting a friend for coffee, reading a good novel or going for a massage, there is something extraordinary in the very ordinary act of going for a walk. Something special and unique, which goes beyond scientific explanation, beyond definition and perhaps even beyond conscious thought. Walking provides a form of connection, not just with the world beyond our offices and homes, but with our thoughts, desires and imagination. When we leave our worries behind, walking reminds us of who we really are.

This feeling of reconnection perhaps stems from the fact that as humans we are perfectly designed and adapted to walk. And although we have now developed far quicker, more 'advanced' ways of moving around, there is a sense in which walking remains – and will always be – the most perfect form of movement. Just as we can't replace foods with vitamin supplements, or sleep with substances that keep us alert, we can't completely replace walking with other forms of transport – at least, not without missing out, or suffering some negative repercussions.

By almost any standard, walking is a slow way of getting around. But that is what makes it so effective and so very necessary. Modern life increasingly flies by so quickly that we barely have time to think or react, leaving us with a perpetual sense of being left behind. And the more we try to keep up, the more stressed and exhausted we become.

In an age where productivity and efficiency reign, walking provides a vital antithesis to the modern world. There is a sense in which it is almost a rebellion, a refusal to be swept mindlessly along by fast culture and faster technology. When we embrace walking as a means of getting around, or of taking time out, we allow ourselves to step off the treadmill for a while (assuming we're not actually walking on a treadmill that is, which is probably the worst place to walk anyway). We assert our right to go at our own pace and in our own direction. And when we walk, rather than rush through life, this enables the mind and body to come together in comfortable synchrony, like the cogs in an old-fashioned clock. The rhythmic pattern of movement creates a kind of mental rhythm too, in which events and thoughts can happen in real time, rather than on fast forward.

Walking is such a radically human activity, that it defies progress and is immune to change. In a world that is constantly evolving, walking reminds us that we are still merely human, that there is still ground beneath our feet. The slap of the soles of our feet on the surface of the earth provides a sense of solidity and permanence when so much about the 21st century feels fake or intangible. Walking takes us out of cyberspace and brings us back down to earth.

When life feels overwhelming or confusing, making a conscious decision to get out for a walk can help us to feel more in control. And when we feel in control, we are less likely to be crushed by negative thoughts and feelings, or to buckle under pressure.

As well as being a powerful prescription for stress, walking is also a huge regulator of emotions. It's amazing how even the foulest or angriest of moods can be appeased by a good walk, or how a gentle stroll can soothe the soul, softening inner pain like salve to a wound. The inherently peaceful nature of walking means it's almost impossible not to experience its pacifying, defusing effect.

And while we can't usually walk away from problems, walking can provide the mental distance we need to deal with challenging situations, buying us time to process our thoughts in a neutral environment. It's as if by changing the view in front of our eyes, we are also able to view the things that trouble or concern us in a different or clearer light, or even to come up with solutions that were previously out of sight.

Often the advice we are given when faced with a difficult decision or situation is to 'sleep on it.' Perhaps an even better suggestion would be to 'walk on it'.

Walk to be healthy,
walk to be happy.

CHARLES DICKENS

walking and mental health – the science bit

When we are active, the brain releases endorphins. These 'feel-good' chemicals reduce pain and stress while helping to raise our mood, creating a natural high, similar to that of morphine, only without the side-effects and the addictive properties. Of course, lots of different types of exercise can trigger this effect, but the great thing about walking is that almost anyone can manage it, there are limitless places to do it, it's free and it doesn't hurt! And because walking raises your heart-rate without sending shockwaves through your chest, it's more likely to relieve stress than cause it. Running, on the other hand, can actually increase the production of the stress hormone cortisol, which is yet another good reason to walk instead.

As well as helping to lower stress levels, numerous studies show that walking reduces the symptoms of depression, and there is evidence that regular physical activity, such as walking, is at least as effective in treating mild to moderate depression as anti-depressants.

A major review led by King's College London, found that engaging in moderate aerobic activity such as brisk walking for just 20 minutes a day cuts the risk of developing depression by one-third. Further large-scale studies have backed up these findings, and there is extensive evidence to show that people who walk regularly are significantly less likely to suffer from depression, and those who have already been diagnosed can ease their symptoms by walking.

What's more, psychologists looking at how exercise relieves anxiety and depression have discovered that going for a walk can enhance your mood even when you don't expect it to – such as when the walk is boring or leads to something you don't want to do. This is thought to be a throwback to evolution, when we moved in order to find food and other rewards, therefore creating a link between movement and positive emotions. In other words, it's hard to understand how much better you will feel after going for a walk, until you actually get up and do it.

As well as bringing about changes in brain chemistry, walking aids positive mental health in many other ways too. For a start, there is the social side of getting out and about, plus the sense of achievement that comes from getting off the couch and pushing yourself a bit further. As an act of self-care, walking can help to raise your self-esteem, and as you achieve your goals, notice your fitness improving or your body changing, this can help boost your self-confidence and motivation, spurring you on to walk further and more often, creating a positive cycle of reinforcement. In short: the more steps you take, the better you feel.

Another powerful benefit of walking during the day is that it can help you to sleep better at night, and getting a good night's sleep is fundamental to both physical and mental health. Furthermore, walking outdoors is a great way to up your daily dose of vitamin D, which is essential for strong bones and general health. Low levels of vitamin D have also been linked to depression. In addition, being outside in natural light can help to protect against seasonal affective disorder (SAD), a type of depression that affects people during the winter months.

If you are in a bad mood, go for a walk. If you are still in a bad mood, go for another walk.

HIPPOCRATES

walking and brain health

One lesser-known benefit of walking is that it can boost cognitive function – that's the rate at which we process information, and our ability to perform various mental activities like reasoning, remembering and problem solving. Walking has been shown to aid all these skills and more – so going for a walk when you're stuck on a problem could be the best way to solve it. What's more, it could even reduce your chances of developing dementia.

In 2017, a Canadian study of more than 1,600 adults aged 65 and older revealed that those who led a sedentary life seemed to have the same risk of being diagnosed with dementia as those who carried a gene mutation predisposing them to the disease. The study, published in the journal of Alzheimer's Disease, suggests that being inactive could raise your dementia risk as much as your genetic make-up – and while you can't change your genes, you can increase the amount you walk.

People with the mutation are three or four times more likely to develop the condition than people without. However, non-carriers can lose their genetic advantage by failing to stay active. Currently, almost 50 million people in the world are living with dementia, and that figure is predicted to rise to 115 million by 2050. And in the absence of any known cure, one of the best things we can do to reduce the odds of developing this horrible disease, or to slow its progress, could be to take up regular exercise, like walking. In addition, further studies have shown that regular walking is associated with better brain function and a reduction in the deterioration of brain tissue as we age.

walking in nature

It has long been recognized that spending time in nature can do wonders for the spirit, at times producing an almost euphoric effect. The first blossom of spring, bright summer skies, the sunset colors of autumn, a robin singing in winter, the quiet determination of flowers growing through cracks in concrete. These every-day miracles are so easy to miss, but so uplifting when we make time for them. And despite the amazing achievements of modern medicine, nature is a source of powerful holistic therapy, with which drugs just can't compete.

Finding contentment and sustenance in nature is nothing new, it's just that in the modern world we have become increasingly secluded from the seasons and the beauty that surrounds us. Yet our predecessors would have felt the energy and the healing power of nature in their bones, way before people started talking about wellness and well-being.

It's only since life has become so enclosed, so manufactured, so synthetic, that we have been forced to re-examine our relationship with the natural world. It's only in shutting ourselves off from the great outdoors – in vehicles and offices and online – that we have realized what we are missing out on, both physically and psychologically. Because just as nature provides us with food and water, it is also a wellspring of happiness and positivity. It's perhaps no coincidence that soaring rates of depression and other mental illnesses have coincided with an increasingly sedentary and indoor existence.

And while we now have science to confirm the rather obvious truth that being in nature makes us feel better, this is something that humans have experienced and written about throughout history. Perhaps one of the loveliest examples is Frances Hodgson Burnett's classic children's novel, 'The Secret Garden' published in 1911, where two thoroughly unpleasant children are transformed by the magic of nature. Of course it's just a story, but there is much truth to be found in fiction. There is now a wealth of evidence to show that spending time in the outdoors and in contact with nature can have an extraordinary effect on mental, as well as physical, health.

What's more, when you go from simply observing or admiring nature, to actually exploring it on foot, the effects are even stronger; leaving us calmer, happier, invigorated and empowered. Research shows that walking, particularly in nature, distracts us from the turmoil inside our heads and decreases rumination – the process of obsessively chewing over the same thoughts. And a reduction in damaging thoughts leads to a more positive outlook and elevated mood.

The blessings of the natural world are universal – mother nature doesn't discriminate – but research has found that the people who benefit the most from exposure to nature are the ones who have the highest risk of developing mental health issues like depression and anxiety in the first place. What's more, studies suggest that exposure to nature can last for seven hours after the experience, so going for an early morning walk or a quick lap of the park before work can leave you feeling happier throughout the day. And if you feel your mood start to wane, just get outside again.

There is now so much evidence linking time spent outdoors with improved mental health, that 'green prescriptions' are increasingly recognized by the medical profession as an effective way of treating symptoms of stress, anxiety and depression. Meanwhile, in Japan, shrinrin-yoku, or 'forest bathing,' is an important part of the country's national public health program. Introduced in the early 1980s, it literally means 'taking in the forest atmosphere', and there is a wealth of scientific literature on the calming and restorative benefits of spending time in a living forest, including lower levels of the stress hormone cortisol and reduced activity in the sympathetic nervous system which triggers the 'fight-or-flight' response associated with fear and stress.

If you look the right way, you can see that the whole world is a garden.

**FRANCES HODGSON BURNETT,
THE SECRET GARDEN**

ten ways to get moving and stay motivated

Once you get into the habit of walking regularly, you will find it hard to stop, as you will soon discover it becomes quite addictive. However, sometimes it can be hard to take those first few steps, especially if you haven't exercised in a while, or are feeling low or burnt out. So here are some small ways to start moving – and most importantly, to keep going.

1. Start small

Forget New Year resolutions – we all know they never make it into February – and set yourself realistic goals instead. Even if it's just walking 10 minutes a day, three times a week, you are much more likely to stick to manageable targets than you are to grandiose ambitions. Starting big can lead to disappointment and a greater chance of giving up. So start small, and work – or walk – up.

2. Make it a habit

The best way to make something a habit is just to keep doing it, ideally at the same time every day, until it becomes such an ingrained part of your life that you can't do without it. Focus on the rewards and find a regular time where walking can slide naturally into your life – whether that's swapping part of your commute for a brisk march, or going for a walk around the block before collapsing onto the couch in the evening.

3. Join a walking group

In addition to all the other benefits of walking, the social side of walking with others can give your mental health an additional boost by helping to foster a sense of community, build friendships and reduce feelings of isolation. This can be so helpful that some doctors and health professionals actually prescribe group walking therapy. What's more, joining a walking group can be a great way of getting to know different routes and exploring new areas. You might also feel safer walking with others than you would alone, especially when it's dark.

4. Ask a friend

If you don't feel like joining a formal group, or can't find one that suits your needs, then why not ask a friend or family member to join you? Committing to walking with someone else can help you to stay motivated and accountable, and of course, they'll benefit too so you'll be doing each other a favor. Walking with a friend or partner is also one of the best ways to strengthen a friendship or relationship. The lack of eye contact as you look ahead rather than at each other, can make it much easier to have deep or difficult conversations. At the same time, your steps will naturally fall in time with each other, and the shared mutual experience of crossing the same ground together can help you to feel more in tune with the person beside you, whether friend or lover.

5. Reward yourself, don't beat yourself up

Walking is a reward in itself, but sometimes promising yourself a treat for reaching your goals can help you to stay focused. Perhaps a movie night after a long weekend hike, or a new pair of walking shoes to put an extra spring in your step. On the other hand, if you have an off-day, or are unwell and don't make it out for a walk, don't give yourself a hard time. Tell yourself tomorrow's another day.

6. Get a dog

This one needs a bit more consideration. Ok, a lot more consideration. But if your lifestyle and environment allows – and you actually like dogs – then getting one for a pet is a pretty guaranteed way to up the amount you walk, often quite dramatically. Of course you will also need to think about vets' bills, insurance, food and the fact you will need to pick up its poo every time you take it for a walk. Don't forget the bags! But if that doesn't put you off, then adopting a four-legged friend is a great way to get fitter and to feel more connected to your community, as dog walking is also a good way to meet people. Although if you opt for a cute or cuddly breed, be prepared for it to be the center of attention every time you leave the house, meaning you may need to allow a bit of extra time for those two miles. Besides helping you to stay fit and active, research suggests that there are many other benefits of having a dog too, including: bringing a sense of meaning and purpose to your life, a reduced risk of depression, less susceptibility to stress and improved immunity and a lower rate of allergies among children. If you are not in a position to take on a pet of your own, then why not ask a friend if you can walk theirs sometimes? There are also websites that hook up dog owners with people who just want to borrow one.

7. Monitor yourself

Some people find it useful to keep a record of how far and how often they've walked. One of the easiest and cheapest ways to do this is just to mark off your walks on a calendar, or to keep an exercise diary in which you can record your progress along with any thoughts or feelings related to walking. And while there is no need to become obsessed with counting steps, some people do find this to be a good incentive. If you don't want to splash out on one of the latest high-tech gadgets, then a simple pedometer will do the job. Remember: use tracking devices wisely, don't let them become the reason for walking and don't let yourself be discouraged if you don't clock up as many steps as you'd hoped.

8. Count the cost

With the rising price of gas, driving isn't just bad for the environment and our health, it's bad for the bank balance too. Why not take a look at all the car journeys you make and work out how much you spend during the course of a week, a month and even a year. Then ask yourself whether you really need to make all those journeys. For example, do you really need to drive the kids to school? Is it essential to use the car every time you run out of milk, visit friends or go to the gym? Ask yourself whether you could walk instead, and how much you could save by doing so. Then think about how you could enjoy the extra money.

9. Set your alarm

Try getting up an hour earlier so you can fit in an early morning stroll before the rush of day kicks in. Many people find this to be an incredibly uplifting way to start the day, leaving them feeling energized and ready to face whatever's ahead. It's easy to assume we are too busy to make time for walking, but often there are ways to free up time. Many of us spend a considerable amount of time doing things that aren't really essential – whether that's idling on social media or doing chores that don't really matter. So forget Facebook and the ironing, and open the front door instead.

10. Keep a walking journal

Whether small or totally memorable, record interesting thoughts you have while on your walk and notes about arresting things you see. In the fullness of time looking back over previous entries will provide a rewarding record of your walks.

A journey of a
thousand miles begins
with a single step.

LAO TZU

did you know?

If enough people swapped just one car journey a week for walking, it would dramatically reduce traffic congestion and prevent thousands of premature deaths from air pollution.

Walking 1 mile (1.6km) in 20 minutes can burn as much energy as swimming for 10 minutes or doing aerobics for 16 minutes.

Walking two miles a day, four times a week, can help you lose up to 1lb (0.5 kg) a month.

You are exposed to more air pollution sitting inside a car than you are walking – even in cities.

If current trends continue, one in five adults around the world will be obese by 2025 – with even higher numbers in developed countries, posing a greater threat to global health than ever before.

If you are seeking
creative ideas,
go out walking.
Angels whisper to
a man when he goes
for a walk.

RAYMOND INMON

CHAPTER 5

walking, mindfulness and creativity

Mindfulness has become something of a buzzword in the last few years, perhaps as a reaction to some of the mindlessness of modern life. In our non-stop, full-throttle world, it's so easy to hurtle from one thing to the next, always thinking ahead or worrying about the past, without fully immersing ourselves in the present. Instead of enjoying the here and now, we remain tangled up inside our heads. Mindfulness provides an antidote to this, and encourages us to let go of unhelpful or negative thoughts and to live in the moment. And this is something we can do while walking.

Mindfulness is a kind of meditation that simply involves focusing your awareness on whatever it is you are doing, as well as on your surroundings. So instead of just operating on autopilot, mindfulness encourages us to consciously pay attention to sensations and experiences we might otherwise miss or take for granted, during seemingly mundane activities such as taking a shower, drinking a coffee or walking to the shops. Bringing awareness to ordinary events enables us to experience life moment by moment, instead of being caught up in worries about the past or fears for the future.

As well as increasing our appreciation of every-day details, mindfulness also interrupts the mind's tendency to dwell on the negative. It helps us to recognize any intrusive or destructive patterns of thinking. The idea isn't to make these negative thoughts disappear, but to accept that they are nothing more than thoughts, and that there is no need to be swept away by them. This can be challenging at first, but with practice, mindfulness can help us to break the chain of unhelpful thinking, so that we can reset our minds and face difficulties more calmly. There is a lot of research demonstrating that mindfulness can help to alleviate and protect against stress, anxiety and mood disorders, and even improve our physical health.

Although meditation and mindfulness are often thought of as sedentary activities, they can be practiced anywhere – including when you are walking. In fact, if you are someone who tends to fidget and finds it hard to remain seated, then mindful walking is a great way to still the mind and step outside your worries at the same time as reaping the physical benefits of being active.

In addition, natural environments provide an ideal setting for mindfulness as they take us away from the hustle and bustle of daily life and the constant buzzing and beeping of electronic devices. Nature heightens the senses, increasing our awareness of the living world – the scent of the earth, the rustle of leaves, the touch of the breeze. And when we stop to smell the roses – or the scent of cut grass, or a eucalyptus tree – we can't help but feel a surge of well-being.

how to walk mindfully

Walking already provides the perfect opportunity to clear the mind, but mindful walking takes things one step further. Being in an outdoor environment sharpens the senses, while the natural, repetitive movement of walking can help shift the mind into an alert but meditative state.

•

Choose a location for your walk – it doesn't matter where, although you might find it easiest to practice mindful walking somewhere peaceful at first. Once you get used to it, you can do it anywhere, such as walking to work or college, or even in a shopping mall. However, to start with, you might prefer to find somewhere quiet and green, such as a park, quiet road or patch of countryside.

•

Begin to walk at a gentle, even pace. Don't worry too much about your arms, just let them swing naturally at your sides, as long as they feel comfortable.

•

As you walk, try to breathe in time with your pace. So you might take two steps as you breathe in and three as you breathe out. Just do whatever feels natural, allowing your breath to unite the mind and body.

•

Now bring your attention to your feet. Instead of just allowing them to steam ahead instinctively, focus on every little detail, from the pressure of the earth on your heel as it meets the ground, to the movement of your foot as it rolls towards the toes, then peels away from the ground and lifts into the air. Feel your weight transfer from one leg to the other, noticing how your muscles contract and your knee bends and your body moves. Then mindfully place your foot back down. You might want to walk slowly at first to really focus on the physical experience of placing one foot down, then the other, taking in every tiny feature and sensation.

•

Now expand your attention to your surroundings, opening your senses to the outside world. Start by noticing the air around you and how it feels: the sun on your back, the wind in your hair, or a cold tingle against your cheeks.

•

Look around, taking in the details of your environment from the cracks in the ground to the colors in the sky. Notice how even when the sky appears monochrome, it's still full of subtle shades and tones.

•

Shift your awareness to your sense of hearing and pay attention to the sounds around you. Does your foot make a noise as it strikes the ground? Can you hear birdsong, or the buzz of insects, or perhaps traffic, voices and sirens? Don't judge these noises, just simply accept them for what they are.

Finally, bring your attention to your sense of smell. Again, just notice any lingering scents, without trying to categorize them as pleasant or unpleasant.

It's completely natural during mindfulness for your mind to wander, and this may happen repeatedly. Don't be hard on yourself; just acknowledge where your mind went and guide your thoughts back to your walk, without feeling bad.

Remember, the more you practice mindful walking, the easier and more natural it will become. And in bringing awareness to this simple, everyday activity, you will find yourself becoming more present and aware in other areas of your life too.

Go out and walk.
That is the glory of life.

MAIRA KALMAN

And forget not that the earth delights to feel your bare feet and the winds long to play with your hair.

KHALIL GIBRAN

barefoot walking

Running around in bare feet is one of those childhood rites of passage, symbolizing freedom, innocence and abandonment. And while parents tend to fret about the risk of stepping on a rock or a bee, and grandparents worry their charges will catch a cold without footwear (they won't), children instinctively love to throw off their shoes at any given opportunity.

By the time we reach adulthood, most of us have forgotten the pleasure of going barefoot. Yet there is no need to be enslaved to socks and shoes just because you are fully grown; walking barefoot can be joyous and liberating at any age. It smacks of non-conformity, and a reconnection with our childhood and our primitive ancestors.

Obviously, it depends on the location – gravel and crowded pavements are best avoided, along with anywhere where there is a risk of sharp objects or dog poo. However, fields, meadows, forests, parks, gardens and beaches all provide wonderful opportunities to feel the ground beneath your feet. Walking barefoot can also add an extra dimension to mindful walking, really helping you to feel a connection with the earth and your own body. So take your shoes off, and maybe throw in a cartwheel for good measure.

All truly great thoughts are conceived while walking.

FRIEDRICH NIETZSCHE

walking and creativity

Most walks have a practical, utilitarian purpose. We walk because we need to get somewhere, or because we want to be healthier or fitter. We walk to burn off calories, or to compensate for the slice of chocolate cake we probably shouldn't have eaten. We walk and walk until we've walked 10,000 steps. And then we stop. We walk because we are told it's good for us. And it is. But there is also a sense in which we have become so obsessed with giving everything we do in life a purpose – the foods we eat, the exercise we take, the ideas we subscribe to – that it's as if we have to justify everything we do. In the current climate of productivity and end-goals, we have forgotten how to walk just for its own sake. Yet there doesn't always need to be a goal.

When we walk without purpose or reason, we enter into a deeper relationship without ourselves – with our thoughts, our senses, our body and our sense of place in the world. Perhaps the most perfect walk is the one that is completely without motive. When we let go of ambition and expectation and just walk, we open ourselves up to all sorts of other possibilities. Walking becomes an existential experience, where we fall into step not just with our surroundings, but with our inner selves, entering an almost hypnotic state. We are simultaneously a part of the earth and a mere dot on the landscape.

Walking provides a window of respite in which we can leave everything behind, both physically and psychologically. Of course, we can and will come back to our schedules, worries and constraints, but when we walk, we can choose to be free. And it's only when we shake off all external influences that we really discover who we are. It's only when we delete all pre-existing thoughts and concerns from our mind that we clear the way for new thoughts and ideas. And it's only when we truly allow our feet to wander without direction that we enable our minds to wander too, providing an open invitation to creativity and the subconscious. And when this happens, we discover that we can walk beyond ourselves, and that walking is as good for the soul as it is for the mind and body.

An early morning walk
is a blessing for the
whole day.

HENRY DAVID THOREAU

I had the best thoughts
in my life in my idle
walks.

DANIEL KAHNEMAN

free thinking

The link between walking and thinking isn't just confined to empirical evidence, but has been investigated by scientists too. In one study, it was found that walking increased creativity by an average of 60 per cent. Researchers at Stanford University looked at a type of creativity called 'divergent thinking' – a thought process or method used to generate creative ideas by exploring many possible solutions. They found that the vast majority of people were more creative while walking than sitting, regardless of where they'd walked, indicating that the physical act of walking is more important than the environment. It was also found that walking-induced creative thinking remained high shortly after sitting back down.

This suggests that sitting at a desk for hours on end isn't just bad for your back and your general health, but mentally stifling, too. In order to get the creative juices flowing, we need to switch off the part of the brain associated with focused thinking and decision-making and allow thoughts to flow freely. In short, we need to make head space. And one of the best ways to do this is to go for a walk. Walking distracts our attention while at the same time relaxes us, creating the perfect environment for inspiration to flow.

In fact, top execs like Richard Branson, Mark Zuckerberg and the late Steve Jobs are all known advocates of the walking meeting. So the next time you are stuck for ideas, or struggling with brain freeze or mental block, your best chance of working out a problem could be to simply get up and walk.

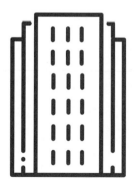

I exist only in the soles of my feet and in the tired muscles of my thighs. We have been walking for hours it seems. But where? I cannot remember.

VIRGINIA WOOLF

There was nowhere to go but everywhere.

JACK KEROUAC

famous walkers

Given the link between creativity and walking, it's little surprise that numerous writers and philosophers have also been avid walkers. From the ancient Greeks to the romantic poets, walking and writing have shared a literary history for centuries. Walking has long provided a way to narrate the world, as well as an opportunity to journey into the mind and become lost in thought. From Victor Hugo to Virginia Woolf, George Orwell to William Wordsworth, Friedrich Nietzsche to Mark Twain, writing and walking have often gone hand in hand. Charles Dickens is said to have routinely walked up to 20 miles a day, once setting out at 2am from his home in London and walking 30 miles to his country residence.

One of the most prodigious walkers was the 19th-century naturalist, essayist and philosopher Henry David Thoreau, who was renowned for taking long walks through the woods and fields, and writing about the plants and animals he encountered. He could easily walk 30 miles in a day, and spent two years living alone in a small cabin in the forest. In one of his most famous essays,

'Walking,' he praises the riches of being immersed in nature, and mourns the invasion of private ownership and its intrusion into the wilderness.

For Thoreau, walking was a spiritual adventure, yet at times even he struggled to remain mindful, confessing: 'I am alarmed when it happens that I have walked a mile into the woods bodily, without getting there in spirit. In my afternoon walk I would fain forget all my morning occupations and my obligations to Society. But it sometimes happens that I cannot easily shake off the village. The thought of some work will run in my head and I am not where my body is – I am out of my senses. In my walks I would fain return to my senses. What business have I in the woods, if I am thinking of something out of the woods?'

If Thoreau could see us now, he would no doubt be appalled at our crippling culture of multi-tasking and agonizing pursuit of goals. He would be horrified to discover that walking – where it takes place at all – has been largely reduced to a set of targets and objectives. Of course, the 21st century is a very different place to the one Thoreau inhabited, and most of us don't have the luxury of being able to spend hours a day lost in nature and in thought. Walking is unequivocally one of the best things we can do to protect and enhance our health, happiness and well-being, and who can argue with objectives like those? But perhaps Thoreau had a point: walking isn't just a means to an end. It is also a path to expansion – of the mind, body and soul. There is a place for the aimless walk, as there is for the purposeful ones.

and finally

Walking is the perfect package of health and happiness. Simple, natural and free, it demands no skill or concentrated effort. There are no rules or instructions, and you can do it wherever you happen to be in the world. Whether for recreation or meditation, solitude or social connection, from infancy to old age, walking is where practicality meets pleasure. As a way of getting around, it leaves no carbon footprint, only real ones. Yet walking takes us way beyond any tangible destination or physical benefit; to walk is to wonder, and the footprints we cast represent our passage through life. Timeless and essential, walking connects us not just to the earth, but to ourselves. To walk is to feel blissfully, wonderfully alive.

Not all those who
wander are lost.

J.R.R TOLKIEN